Love,
Karla & Hillary

Kzemler @ att.net

Hillary
Goes To
The White House

Karla Lee Zemler

the small press

Hillary Goes to the White House

The Small Press
16250 Knoll Trail Drive, Suite 205
Dallas, Texas 75248
www.BBSmallPress.com
(972) 381-0009

ISBN 978-1-612548-08-1
Library of Congress Control Number 2011961736
Printed in the United States of America
10 9 8 7 6 5 4 3 2 1

Author contact information:
Karla Lee Zemler
HillaryGoesToTheWhiteHouseBook@gmail.com

DEDICATION
To Lori, Vivian & Martin
To all the dogs in my life and in the world

TRIBUTE TO JOHN DENVER
Then I look in the center
Suddenly everything's clear
I find myself in the sunshine and my dreams

A SPECIAL THANK YOU
Jenny Meadows, Editor
Donna Aldridge, Designer
Rebecca Wright, Publicist
Shirley Richardson, Publicist
Zeke Jarzemsky, The Black Lab

HILLARY GOES TO THE WHITE HOUSE

My name is Hillary Rambunctious Cocker, which is a big name for such a small dog. I did not realize how big it was until I saw it on my registration papers. I knew I must be important with a name like that.

Seeing my name was the first step in my awakening to who I am and what my destiny is meant to be. I believe we all have a purpose. It is our job to search deep inside for who we are so we can find the puppy we are meant to be.

Always remember, you can do anything when you know who you are and when you know you are deeply loved. I love you and I will lick your face to prove it.

The second step in my awakening was to realize how much I love the big guy, you know, the Big Dog in Heaven, the one who loves us all equally. Some people tell me I am dyslexic and the word is God (not Dog) in Heaven. I am a puppy now, but some day I will be a big dog, and I believe the Big Dog is a Dog because he or she wants me to relate to someone who looks like me. Whichever you prefer, Dog or God, that's the one in Heaven who created all creation and loves us no matter our nose size, hair color, breed, or whether we are fully potty trained.

Back to my story. *I dogress...*

I realized that I had love in my heart that I wanted to share with everyone else. I took a long, long, long nap and dreamed, dreamed, dreamed that one day I would be able to follow a scent that would lead me to my destiny, the destiny that fit my big name, Hillary Rambunctious Cocker.

I love my name. Because my mom says it so lovingly, my chest swells and it makes me want to be my best and do my best. I love being with my parents, playing chase, rolling in the grass, chewing bones, and just hanging out. I feel loved when my parents are around. I feel secure and confident. I absorb their love and it makes me stronger.

I was dreaming, dreaming, dreaming, and then it happened. I found my destiny. I could not believe it. It was just a word that hit my heart and made me want to sing.

Some say my singing sounds like howling, but it is the song in my heart. I sing my song and everyone needs to sing the song in his or her heart, no matter how it sounds to anyone else. It was my word, made just for me, and it made me sing.

The word was *Pawliticks*. Of course, the end of the word scared me!! Ticks scare all puppies and doggies. My destiny was to go into pawliticks. I will explain. The Big Dog loves us and gave us families and friends. With these friends we built packs and formed communities. Then we formed a government to protect and support people to live in harmony with others. That is why it is "Government for the people and by the people."

When I got my word, my heart swelled, my little tail wiggled and waggled, and I rolled in the grass. I was one happy puppy. I wanted to love and serve everyone, even big, mean, scary dogs. Did you know that mean dogs are just scaredy cats (funny, isn't it?) who live with a lot of fear? The same with you people with only two paws. The meaner

they are, the more afraid they are, and the more we have to put our paws together and pray for them.

Back to my beautiful word, pawliticks. Back to ticks scaring me. Ticks are little pests that bite you and suck life energy out of you. Mom says in pawliticks, I would meet a lot of ticks along the path. I would have to be brave and strong to follow my convictions. She said they get so busy biting at nice doggies that I might get distracted. I might be so busy scratching that I might give up. We get flea and tick medicine from the vet. Maybe the pharmaceutical companies could develop a medicine to repel people who are like fleas and ticks.

Mom also said I have to be careful of my *faupaws*. She said I would have to watch my steps because everyone would be looking for my faupaws and jump on them like a cat on catnip. I counted my paws: 1, 2, 3, faupaws. I guess I could get into a lot of trouble with faupaws. I might bark too loud, run too fast, and really mess up. I looked at my faupaws, and I knew every day I would have to ask the Big Dog to bless my faupaws and to let me use them wisely.

Pawliticks means that you extend your paw to help everyone else. Mom says that I will have to be courageous to not be hurt by their bites. She said they might do something as silly as make fun of my hair!!

I have thick hair and it goes a lot of different directions all at the same time. How silly that they would focus on my hair when I have such long, luscious ears, great intellect, persistence, and a desire to help all dogs and people. Why, why, why would they focus on the little stuff? It hurts my feelings, and it isn't nice. Didn't their parents love them and bite their ears when they were biting others too hard? Didn't their parents teach them the dogma of our country, which centers around love and respect for every creature?

My special word "Pawliticks" is too big and beautiful to be made into a dog fight. How can they call me a yellow dog democrat? Are they color blind? Can't they see I am chocolate and white? This seems like *apawling* behavior on their part. As you can see, I have been feeling a great deal of confusion and frustration over how my word could be so abused and doggone destroyed.

I took a long, long, long nap, and when I awoke I was back on track. I decided I was right. Pawliticks was designed for people and dogs to speak. Apparently, dogs have been better trained to speak than people. I guess they don't teach people's kids to speak, speak, speak, and then get a treat. When I am *Presidog*, I will make sure all people and dogs exercise their right to speak.

I heard there was a voting issue, too. I pledge that every vote will be counted, if it takes the dog days of summer to accomplish it. You can't teach everyone to speak and then not count their votes. Isn't it supposed to be life, liberty, and the pursuit of happiness (naps, bones, and playing) for everyone?

ON THE TRAIL, MAKING CONTACT

I decided to call some people on my mom's *I-pawd* phone. It is really cool, but dialing with my big furry paws isn't the easiest thing to do. And texting is almost *impawsible*.

I called a guy named Mr. Bush. I thought for sure he would be an environmentalist with a name like that. He said his daddy was in oil and that made it difficult to be an environmentalist. I said, "Too bad." It was kind of a short conversation.

I thought all bushes were here to purify the air through photosynthesis, which makes the world a better place. I guess some bushes don't get to follow their destiny. When I am Presidog, I will make sure that no one is kept on a leash that holds them back from their true essence. Essence is that feeling inside when you love who you are.

YOU KNOW THAT NO MATTER HOW PEOPLE TREAT YOU, IT IS A REFLECTION OF THEM, NOT YOU. THEIR BEHAVIOR TELLS US THEY DON'T FEEL GOOD INSIDE IF THEY DON'T TREAT PEOPLE WITH RESPECT.

Because Mom had more minutes, I made another call. I hoped there would be roaming charges; we doggies like to be able to roam from here to there and back to here. We pick up our emails by the sidewalk left in the grass.

I called another guy. He said his name was Anonymous. Kind of a strange name, I thought. He said all the fat cats have all the money, licking their dirty little paws, ignoring everyone else. Those cats sure do have ignoring down to a fine art. I was so doggoned appawled that I had to go outside and eat some grass and throw up.

I called one more guy. His name was Dick. No, not Dick from Dick and Jane. He just did not sniff out right. Someone said he was bright, but he did not use his talents the way the Big Dog intended. The Big Dog says from those who receive much, much is expected. Translation: If you are given much, you are supposed to give much, not take, silly! I heard they will need a big scooper to clean up the messes he left behind.

I went away feeling *dogpressed*, but I knew I was being tested. All this pain and disillusionment, Mom says, would help me find my wisdom to be the best Presidog ever. So I took a long, long, long, long nap and chewed some bones to sharpen my canines. I knew I was going to need all my strength to follow my heart and stay on my path so I could help all the people and puppies.

I awoke refreshed and ready to venture forth. I looked into a book written by my friend Al. I decided we were friends because we have similar ideas. His ideas are slightly more complicated than mine. He talked to me through his book about relativity and double

E concepts. Not everyone can interpret his material like I can, so I will explain what I came away with.

On the theory of relativity: We Are All Related. There is no difference between me and you. Some of us are hairier. Some of us have shorter tails than others. We are all different colors until you stick out your tongue, and then we are all a beautiful pink inside, which is the color of love. We are all the same color inside, and our insides are the most important part of who we are. If someone makes fun of your outside, they don't know who they truly are.

When we forget the theory of relativity, we really get lost. No matter how long you put your nose to the ground and sniff, you will always be off the path.

For every action there is a reaction. This translates to What You Do Matters. You get away with nothing. Think about the impact you are having before you do it. This will help you keep your nose clean.

Back to my friend Al and his theory about double E—no, not electrical engineering—Empathy and Equality. These are the two critical compounds that create a loving world, which translates to world peace. When everyone is our equal, we don't try to dominate other people. In doggy terms, that is *Alpha dog* stuff. Domination stems from insecurity and fear.

My mom says I dogress a lot, so let me get back to my big plan.

MY SPECIAL PLAN FOR YOU

Now I want to share My Special Plan. I hid it somewhere in the backyard with some bones. I know some people will have a few bones to pick with me when I reveal my plan. I'm not sure why everyone can't sit and stay. You don't have to roll over or anything. Let's listen to each other, so we can take the ticks out of pawliticks.

Think of My Special Plan as something that will make you feel special. Like when people tell you that you are special, and you feel all warm inside. It makes me want to wiggle all over. When people deep down in their soul know that they are special, they look at everyone else and realize they are just as special.

You ask what Special stands for. You want to know that I am not some silly little puppy chasing her own tail, barking up the wrong tree, or just leaving a big pile of you-know-what. You want to know I have a plan and that I will get in that big dog fight and get your bones back.

I hear that in the United States, some people have other people's bones (I think you call it money; funny, it doesn't sound like it tastes very good) and you want someone to fight for you. I'm your puppy. With all of us working together you will see happy tail-wagging times again.

HERE IS MY SPECIAL PLAN

SOCIETY: This includes what we need to live in harmony together: safe places to live, good vets (*I think you call it health care for all*), a healthy environment, and services to take care of old dogs and doggies who need extra assistance (*everyone counts*)

PEACE: Peaceful communication—internal peace and world peace

EDUCATION: Good education for all; an educated population cannot be tricked by fat cats or bully-dogs

CO-OPERATIONS: Places where people work together, where they are treated well and respected, and bring home the bones

INTERNATIONAL COMMUNITY: We are all in this together, and we want to be friends with our neighbors

ACCOUNTABILITY: We will be financially and legislatively responsible by making good decisions, looking at long-term impact, and I will take a bite out of pork-barrel spending (*who gave a vote to the pigs, anyway?*)

LEGISLATION: For the people, by the people; not for or by special interests

Yes, we will have a strong military.

I like carrying a big stick, except when I try to go through the doggy door and get stuck. One time, I got a stick that was three feet long through the doggy door. Mom was so proud of me. She kept saying, "Look at this mess!! Look at this mess!!" I'm not sure what a mess is, but it must be really good. I didn't tell her it took me half a day and a long nap to accomplish this big exciting "mess."

After *Candidogs* go around the country sharing their plans, then the big race is on.

May the best *puppy* win.

MOM SAYS CLEAR YOUR THROAT FIRST SO YOU DON'T HAVE
A FROG IN IT (I WASN'T GOING TO EAT THE FROG).

MOM SAYS A SMART MAN SAID TO BARK SOFTLY AND CARRY A BIG STICK.

THINGS DO NOT ALWAYS TURN OUT THE WAY
WE EXPECT, BUT IT IS ALWAYS OK

Well, well, well, the best laid plans of mice and men, and puppies too. I had my plan. I ran the race of my life. I ran and ran and ran as hard and fast as I could. I think I came in second; not bad for a little girl pup on her first try.

At first, I felt defeated, so I licked my wounds, my paws, and my bowl clean. A full stomach makes me feel loved and makes me think clearer and smarter.

I cried a little. Actually, a lot. I even tried to howl, but everyone said I looked a little silly. It takes a lot of practicing to be good at howling. I didn't know that, so I kept crying until I felt better. Once you get all those tears out, even though it is hard to let yourself cry (trying to be a big dog and all), you will feel much better.

I had a lot of questions to sort out in my mind. I kept asking myself, "Was I barking up the wrong tree? Did the Big Dog really lead me all this way to land me on this little stump of a tail?"

By the way, did you hear? Stump, a 10-year-old spaniel, won the Westminster Kennel Club Best in Show in 2009. Who says you can't teach an old dog new tricks?

His story gives me inspiration. Maybe, just maybe, I could be the comeback kid and run this race again.

Before I could go forward again, though, I knew I had to get my tail wrapped around what just happened. I wanted to learn from my mistakes. I did not want to be chasing my tail in circles I had run before. Everyone says I am smarter than that. They say that if you don't reflect on where you have been and what you have done, you might find yourself in déjà vu all over again.

You want to work really hard in school so you don't repeat the same grade. It's the same idea. Yet it is OK if you need to repeat a grade level. Be proud of yourself for making sure you have learned everything you need for the next step in school and in life.

I decided I couldn't find the answer inside of me, so I put my paws together and prayed, "Why, why, why, why me, Big Dog?" It felt kind of like whining, but that was where I was starting out. I didn't get an answer, so I figured the Big Dog didn't like the question.

OK, OK! I decided to try again. "Why did it feel like you put me on a leash and you were leading me all this way and it was really going so well? I met so many people I liked. I listened to their sad stories and how much they believed in me. Given the chance, I knew I could help them. I wanted to help them with all my heart. I wanted to lick their faces and tell them everything would be OK."

Someone, I don't remember who, said that was probably not a good idea. But I dogress.

"Big Dog, you led all this way for what purpose? To hurt my feelings? To make me look small (I kind of am already small)? So people could gleefully say, 'See, a girl can't win'? I can accept that the race is over. I just need to understand."

Then it all made sense. I realized what my question needed to be.

"PLEASE HELP ME UNDERSTAND THE PURPOSE OF THIS PART OF MY JOURNEY SO I CAN GROW, BE STRONGER, AND BE A BETTER PUPPY."

There it was again; the Big Dog was giving me the answer inside my head. The Big Dog wanted me to be a stronger and better puppy. It would somehow prepare me for my future in ways I could not understand until I arrived at the future.

I felt so relieved. The Big Dog was not playing tricks on me. I was building more character. Sometimes, actually a lot of time, actually all the time, building character is hard work. It gets developed when you stand up for what is right when it is not popular, and when you stand up for people or doggies who cannot stand up for themselves.

Also, when you listen to that inner voice that says, "You know what is right." That voice that says, "Are you going to ignore me this time?"

When you get to the other side of character-building, you feel a sense of peace and self-acceptance that comes from listening to your inner puppy. This feeling doesn't happen when you do the easy thing, when you take advantage of someone else, or when you tell a lie. That feeling is like a rock in your gut. Mom says listen to your heart of hearts and you will keep your paws clean.

All this work—running the race of my life and putting all these pieces together—really wore me out, so I took a long, long nap. Puppies can really sleep a lot, if you haven't noticed. You probably do not know why we sleep so much. Well, I will let you in on a little doggie secret.

We doggies worry a lot about you people. You seem to chase your tails more than we do, which seems pretty funny from our perspective.

We see you stressed out over many things that are not important. You chase all that green stuff and then buy all that stuff you do not need.

The truth is, all the green you will truly ever need is right in your own back yard. There's no place like home, there's no place like home. We call that *puppy love*, hanging with your pack.

I finished my long nap, and I stretched and stretched and stretched and felt so much better. I think it's called Yoga. Whatever, it is good for the soul.

HOW DID THAT HAPPEN?

I just have to tell you about the Lab who beat me in the race of my life. He is truly a Bow Wower. He is sleek, smart, well groomed, and well spoken. His motto is speak softly, carry a big smile, and wag that tail. He sure does know how to wag that tail to get things done. I do not actually know if he is a Lab or not, but he has the energy of a Lab.

He is a nice guy. I would love to not like him, but I cannot help liking him. If anyone was going to beat me, I am glad it was this guy. Truth be told, I was going to make him my *Vice Presidog*, pick of the litter. Did I mention he has the most adorable family you would ever want to meet?

The Big Dog works in mysterious ways. I had said I wanted to help everyone, and do you know what this nice guy, BarkO, did for little ol' me? I wanted to help everyone, and he asked me to be Secretary of State for the United States of America. Me!! Yes, me!!! I did not realize this is how I could help everyone while BarkO was primarily focused on the people of the United States.

Isn't the Big Dog amazing? He knows better than we do what our heart truly desires. Of course, I had an issue with the word "Secretary." It put my snout out of joint for a few days. People are always trying to tell little girl puppies, "You would make a great secretary, sweetie." Yuck!! I had to keep saying, "of State, of State." Then "Secretary" was not so bad. Why don't they call it CEO of State?

I was absolutely honored by BarkO's offer and affirmation of my commitment to serve. I think I will enjoy letting him be my boss. He wants everyone to speak, speak their mind. You know we puppies like to speak, speak, speak. God gave me a big, imaginative mind and I like to share it, because that is what we are supposed to do for the common good.

Guess what. I get to go to the United Nations, which is not the same thing as the Westminster Kennel Club. It can look similar, especially when you see how some of these pups grandstand and walk around with their noses in the air. (The United Nations is where all the Top Dogs, or people, gather to solve all the big problems of the world.) I look forward to working with the German Shepherd, the Australian Sheepdog, the Newfoundland, the French Poodle, the English Spaniel, Irish Setter, and all the smart dogs from other countries.

The purpose of the United Nations is to recognize that we are truly all from the same pack. We do not look alike or think alike, but we are all in this game together, and if one of us loses, we all lose. Everyone has something to teach us, if we keep our minds open to learning and our paws on the floor, unless, of course, we have been invited up for a hug.

Mr. BarkO wants the world to be a better place, and we all have to sit up and ask what we can do to help. President BarkO said he needed a smart dog with a good nose and a big heart to be his Secretary of State. He picked little ol' me. It made me feel like crying again, which is OK. These were happy tears. I wanted to put my big paws around him and give him a hug. He wanted to shake hands. We puppies are big into shaking hands, just like you people. Maybe I will get a treat when I do some great things for our country and the world.

My mission is to work on world peace, clean water for everyone (no one wants dirt in their bowl), clean air, and fighting disease and hunger (no one can be a happy puppy and run and play all day if their belly is not full). All children should have safe places to live and schools where they can learn.

Did you know you can help? Agencies like World Vision help children go to school, build schools, and supply farm animals so children can have eggs and milk through donations from families like yours. You could get your class to sponsor a child or raise money to build a school. Ms. Oprah does a lot of charity work too. You could write her and see if you could help her.

You can also help out at home. Your home is a community that needs everyone to work as a team to get everything accomplished. Someday you will have puppies, and you will want them to help out, so do your chores and your homework without being asked a million times. If parents spend all their energy barking at us, they have less energy to play with us.

I need to wrap up my tail for now. I am going off to serve all of you and our country. We are so blessed in this country to live freely (except when we need to be on a leash, for safety) and to have the freedom to be who we are and to vote for people who will serve all the people.

Thank you for listening. And remember—I believe in you, your parents believe in you, and you should always believe in yourself. Do what your heart of hearts tells you, and you will find your purpose and be one happy puppy, like me. This is the end of my tail for now.

HIllary is a four-year-old cocker spaniel who lives with her mom (a psychotherapist) in Dallas along with the rest of her family. Hillary believes people would not need psychotherapy if they had puppies in their lives. Please donate to charities and agencies that support the health and happiness of children and pets. Fifty percent of the author's profits from this book will be dispersed to help two- and four-legged children.

You can email Hillary at
HillaryGoesToTheWhiteHouseBook@gmail.com.

"Peace and Love"

Debra is a Dallas-based Photographer and Videographer. Throughout her 21-year career she has produced images for National and local ad campaigns, brochures, magazines, and videos for various companies and corporations.

"Each individual is unique in their own special way . . . I take time to capture their essense of self."